Epilepsy Book For kids

by Layla Reid

© Mark and Sarah Reid 2012

ISBN 978-1-3999-0290-8

No part of this publication may be reproduced, stored in a retrieval system, or transmitted, in any form or by any means, electronic, mechanical photocopying, recording or otherwise, without the prior permission of the publisher and copyright holder.

All rights reserved

Printed and bound in the UK

The publishers would like
to thank

Epilepsy Action, Epilepsy Society
and
Young Epilepsy

for their advice and support
in the creation of this book.

Hello, my name is Layla and my mummy has epilepsy. Maybe your mummy, daddy or someone else in your family has epilepsy. I hope this book will let you know what to do if they have a seizure.

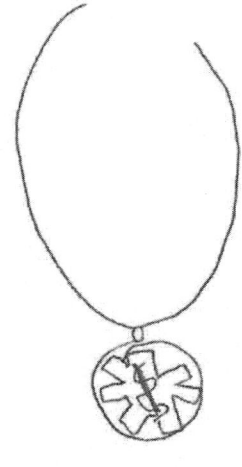

My mums special necklace

My Mummy wears a special necklace to tell people she has epilepsy. I show this to adults who help her when she has a seizure.

Sometimes my mummy has seizures where she gets very confused and struggles to speak. I know she needs help. I help mummy to sit down and call daddy to come and help. I keep calm and reassure mum "it's ok mummy."

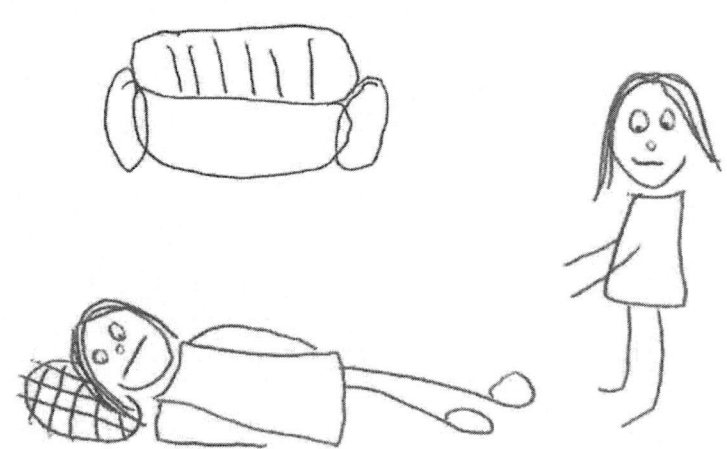

Sometimes my mummy has seizures where she falls to the ground and shakes. I call for an adult. Then I reassure mummy and put something soft under her head. When the seizure has finished the adult will put mummy on her side in the recovery position.

When my mummy has a seizure I try to move things out of the way that might hurt her. I never put anything in her mouth and I never give her a drink or food.

IF I cant Find an adult, I know how to call 999 for an ambulance. My Mummy put a list of Phone numbers by the Phone so I can call For our Family or an ambulance For help.

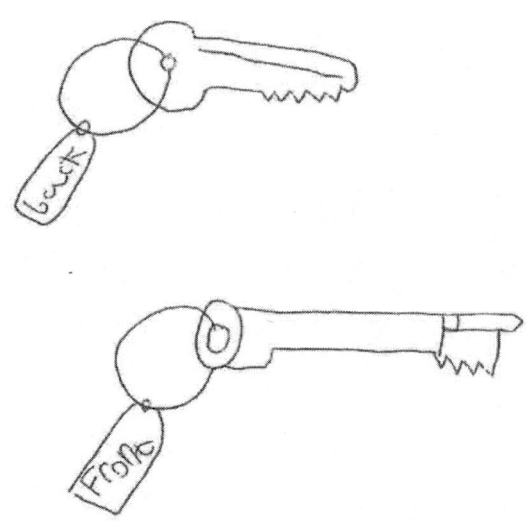

My mummy has written Front door and Back door on her keys so I can let the ambulance people in to look after Mummy.

Mummy only cooks when daddy is home because she might have a seizure and we dont want to have a fire.

When Mummy baths me daddy is always home in case she has a seizure.

When mummy has a shower she <u>always</u> takes the bath plug out in case she has a seizure. She doesn't take baths only showers. She only has a shower when daddy is at home.

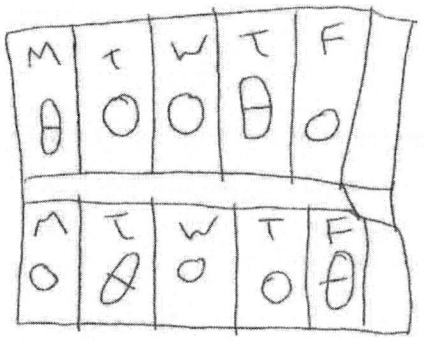

Every morning and night Mummy must always take her tablets — but I must never touch them or I would be <u>very</u> poorly.

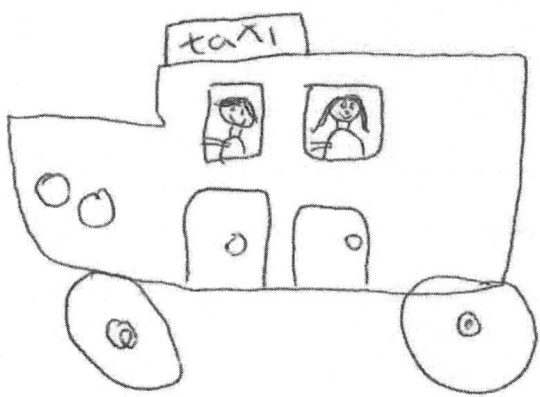

Mummy does not drive at the moment but she has a special bus pass and a taxi takes her to work.

When my brother or sister comes I will teach them how to look after Mummy too.

Further information on
many aspects of epilepsy
can be found at the following websites:

Epilepsy Action
www.epilepsy.org.uk

Epilepsy Society
www.epilepsysociety.org.uk

Young Epilepsy
www.youngepilepsy.org.uk

EPILEPSY First Aid

Stay Safe Side

Do

1. Remain calm

2. Keep the person safe from harmful objects

3. Look at a watch and time the seizure

4. Make the person as comfortable as possible

5. When seizure end Turn the person onto their side

6. If seizure more than 5 minutes call 911

7. Stay with them until they awake

Do Not

1. Do not panic

2. Do not restrain

3. Do not put anything in their mouth

Made in the USA
Monee, IL
03 May 2026

49449665R00020